HAL•LEONARD
VIOLIN
PLAY-ALONG

Johann Strauss, Jr.

CONTENTS

Jon Vriesacker, violin
Audio arrangements by Peter Deneff
Recorded and Produced by Jake Johnson
at Paradyme Productions

ISBN 978-1-4803-5099-1

HAL•LEONARD®
CORPORATION
7777 W. BLUEMOUND RD. P.O. BOX 13819 MILWAUKEE, WI 53213

In Australia Contact:
Hal Leonard Australia Pty. Ltd.
4 Lentara Court
Cheltenham, Victoria, 3192 Australia
Email: ausadmin@halleonard.com.au

Visit Hal Leonard Online at
www.halleonard.com

Artist's Life

By Johann Strauss, Jr.

Blue Danube Waltz

By Johann Strauss, Jr.

Emperor Waltz

By Johann Strauss, Jr.

Kiss Waltz

By Johann Strauss, Jr.

Pizzicato Polka

By Johann Strauss, Jr.

Tales from the Vienna Woods

By Johann Strauss, Jr.

Wine, Women and Song

By Johann Strauss, Jr.

Thousand and One Nights

By Johann Strauss, Jr.